The Secrets to Long-Lasting Relationships

A Guide to Keeping Love Alive

Judy C Foster

Table of Content

INTRODUCTION

Once upon a time, there was a young man named John who had just moved to a new city. He was hoping to start fresh and find a new life for himself. He was eager to explore and find out what the city had to offer, but he was also a little apprehensive.

One day, while out exploring the city, he stumbled upon a small café with a beautiful mural painted on its walls. He was immediately drawn to it and decided to go inside. He ordered a cup of coffee and took a seat at a small table near the window. His gaze was drawn to the mural again and he couldn't help but admire the vibrant colors and intricate details.

Suddenly, a woman walked in and sat down at the table next to him. She had a warm, inviting smile and the two of them quickly started talking. They talked about their lives, their dreams, and their pasts.

John felt a connection to her that he had never experienced before.

As the conversation went on, John realized he was falling in love with this woman. They started seeing each other regularly, and soon enough they were in a committed relationship. They had found each other and were in love.

John and his partner were deeply in love, but they knew it wasn't going to be easy. They faced challenges and struggles, but they never stopped loving each other and finding ways to keep the flame alive. They went on romantic dates, shared intimate moments, and always made sure to show each other how much they cared.

Years passed and their love only grew stronger. Even when life got tough and they faced difficult times, they were able to lean on each other and keep the love alive.

John and his partner had found each other and found true love. They had found a way to keep their love alive and it was a beautiful thing.

What is crucial in a relationship? Everything! Genuine connections are the foundation of true success. Everything less is only surface-level.

Based on relationships, you buy and sell. Relationships play a role in who you hire and fire. Based on your relationships, you might concur or disagree.

You need relationships for any project you do. Why do you (and I) consistently screw up relationships when you are aware of their importance?

When was the last time you conducted a relationship inventory? Or do you only believe that the "health" of your relationship will endure?

You anticipate a relationship to last when you enter one, right? Regrettably, both people and things change throughout time. People's weaknesses eventually come to the surface, and you find yourself maintaining relationships more often than you'd like. What time do you cut the power? Should you unplug the device? What time do you clean your home? Your next step is determined by what?

You should evaluate the worth of your connection at this time. A healthy relationship is like a wonderful pair of shoes; when they're brand new, they're clean, shiny, and stylish. After that, people feel wonderful and are really at ease. After some time, they begin to appear a little worn out; there may even be a little tear or two, and the sole needs to be repaired.

While beginning a new relationship, we frequently develop an unconscious expectation of how much upkeep this bond will require. Generally, if we give it some attention, we may examine this idea under a microscope since it is still in its infancy.

Yet, time is a commodity and, in your hot little hands, is worth as much as a trillion dollars. We try to conserve it, divide it up across numerous jobs, squander it, and take it for granted. But, the majority of us seldom consciously link relationship upkeep with time.

It cannot be disputed that when a new relationship first begins, both partners seek one another for their wants to be met. If neither party provides sufficient upkeep, the other will eventually withdraw unless a clear understanding is communicated at the outset.

So how do we decide how much of our time we should devote to potential relationships?

It just depends on how strong of a foundation you want them to have. I desire a strong foundation for all of my relationships. Your value system should be built around sacrificing the upkeep of other relationships.

CHAPTER 1

Fundamentals of Relationship Resolution

Many of us aspire to have good relationships, but it may be darn difficult.

It can be challenging to navigate the emotions, needs, wants, hangups, and a never-ending stream of the bizarre behavior of two very different people. Making some relationship resolutions, though, might be beneficial. You know, it helps to check in occasionally to make sure everyone is having a good time.

Remember that love partnerships are supposed to enhance our lives. But, that does not imply that they are labor-free. The notion that relationships should be simple if they are "good" is absurd and raises our expectations.

The following are the most fundamental but unquestionably crucial considerations you must make when making relationship resolutions. Start by following them to establish the best connection ever!

What Is Basic

Your past year likely contained both good and bad things, joy and pain, victories and disagreements, if you are like the majority of couples in today's society.

Why not take some time now that a new year has begun to say goodbye to and let go of all the negative things that occurred in your relationships last year? Spend only a few minutes talking with your partner about the greatest methods to improve your current relationship above what it was.

The key is forgiveness.

You both must forgive and put the past behind you so that you may go ahead into the new year with a positive outlook. Now is the ideal time to let things go and embrace the idea of forgiveness if you have been holding a grudge against your ex-partner for a while and find it difficult to forgive them.

Refusing to forgive may be likened to a poison that gradually seeps through your entire existence, filling it with such bitterness and finally driving a gap between the two of you. If you forgive your partner, it does not imply that you approve of what they did. More significantly, forgiving someone signifies that you have finally attained peace with them to move on.

A Must is Issue Assessment

Take some time to consider your relationship's main issues. This may be a result of poor communication for some people. Others may be dealing with money problems or a wide range of other challenges. Talk about the issue and consider how you might make improvements. To ensure that you both have an equal say in the choice, pay attention to one another's ideas.

The Better for Change

Discuss how you two can make the positive aspects of your relationship even better. Each couple's relationship has its unique strengths. Talk about these issues and use them as evidence that you two are proceeding appropriately.

Make a promise to yourself not to ever take the positive qualities of your relationship for granted as you talk things out to make good things even better.

Discuss romance and intimacy.

When we talk about romance, we should also talk about your sexual life. There is no disputing that this is a crucial element of your relationship, so be careful not to ignore it. Have a good time and play about with this. Consider strategies to improve and make this aspect of your relationship more enjoyable.

Consider what to anticipate in the upcoming year.

Do you intend to start a family this year or buy your own home? Perhaps the greatest time to begin making preparations is this New Year. Most likely, the two of you want to get healthier and fitter. You can do it jointly since it might be enjoyable to accomplish a goal you have set for yourself in this way.

Discuss your goals for the coming year with your partner, then look for ways to support them.

Encourage them and aid one another in achieving your goals. Naturally, it's crucial to grow as a person when in a relationship because you'll be happy there if you're at your best.

Organize and prepare meals together. Hold hands as you stroll together. Having each other this New Year is the best gift you can give to your partner, regardless of whatever plans you may have.

CHAPTER 2

Prioritize Your Well-being.

Some people eventually stop caring about themselves once they enter a relationship. But for a relationship to succeed, each partner must understand how to look after themselves. That way, they can better look after one another. Learn the value of putting your needs first before anything else.

You alone deserve your love and affection more than anybody else in the universe.

The Secret to a Healthy Relationship is Self-Care

When in a relationship, looking after yourself is just as crucial as looking after the partnership. You must first take care of yourself before attempting to mend your relationship. You can use the proverb that goes, "You can never give away something that you do not have," in this situation. You won't ever have a joyful and peaceful relationship until you first feel happy and at peace.

The likelihood is that you will plunge headfirst into the depths of your dysfunctional relationship if you decide to forego these precautions. This is the reason you need to take all the necessary steps to steady yourself before letting things get to your head.

You must first do the following actions to improve your chances of success before tackling the relationship's fundamental flaws.

Ensure Your Well-Being No Matter What Happens Along the Road

Commit yourself that no matter what happens in your relationship, you will continue to take care of yourself and be okay.

You will feel helpless and afraid once your happiness solely depends on your lover being by your side at all times. As a result, it will be more likely that you will resort to ineffective behaviors like pleading and begging.

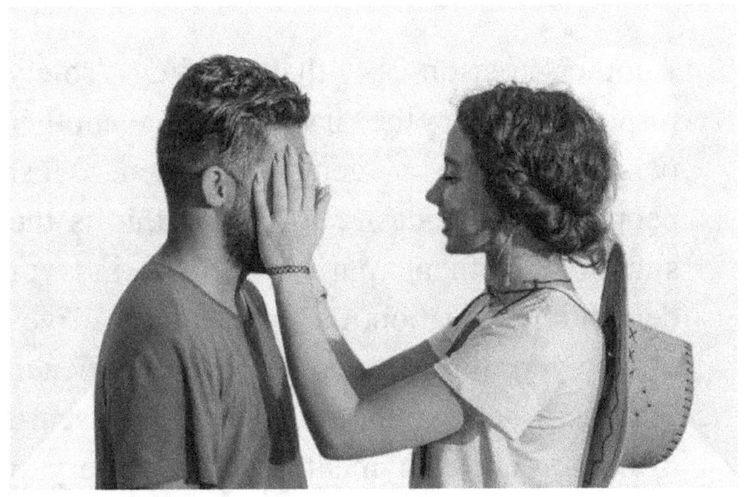

The more frequently this occurs, the less likely it is that your partner will want to continue the relationship. How come?

Your partner will perceive you as someone who is emotionally reliant and dependent on them, which is a reasonable cause for this. You will always have higher expectations of others, therefore no matter what they do for you, it won't be enough for you. Your spouse will not be able to escape it, and it will cause him or her to fear being overwhelmed by your constant requests for care and attention.

Another reason is that feeling solely responsible for the happiness of another person can be a genuine burden. Most people feel the desire to flee if this is the situation. When put in this kind of demanding situation, the spouse who strives to be everything to another can experience bitterness and wrath, smothering any sense of humor and enjoyment that is necessary to establish a lasting relationship.

You will undoubtedly come from a position of strength and empowerment when you value and believe in your ability to thrive, whether you are in a relationship or alone.

These two qualities can draw admiration from others and inspire respect, which will make you a more appealing and devoted companion.

Despite Feeling Miserable, Make the Commitment to Continue Living a Happy Life.

You don't need to wait till your relationship is ideal to organize some enjoyable things to do on your own. If you'd like, you can enroll in lessons to learn fun hobbies like playing the guitar or fine-dining cookery. Make a list of the sites you want to visit in your neighborhood and those nearby. Acquire new abilities, stand out, and expand your sphere of influence.

You'll feel a lot better and even happier with yourself while you're having fun and staying active. Also, this will improve your partner's perception of your attractiveness.

Regardless of the health of your relationship, you will improve the likelihood that your spouse will want to spend more time with you when you live your own life with passion, adventure, and self-care.

CHAPTER 3

Learn to be more accepting of uncertainty.

If one party is constantly skeptical of the other's words, feelings, and behavior, no relationship will flourish and succeed. A so-called "benefit of the doubt" mindset can significantly aid in reorienting your relationship in the best manner.

Love decides to have optimistic views of other people. It assumes the best and protects them. It does not make unfavorable assumptions to cover up the unknowns. And love makes every effort to deal with them and move on when our worst fears come true.

Assume the best about your partner

Have you ever made a significant negative impact on your relationship by doing something stupid, foolish, or hurtful? Practically everyone in the world has likely wounded someone they care about, whether on purpose or accidentally. In reality, studies have shown that many people in long-term relationships will intentionally damage their significant other.

There will inevitably be disagreements in every partnership. If you know someone well enough and have been with them for a long enough time, eventually something will happen that will cause stress, whether it be bewilderment, misunderstandings, or conflicts.

Individuals will annoy, enrage, disappoint, hurt, or disturb you. There is no way around this because your companion is a human being just like you. Will you react angrily in such circumstances or will you give your partner the benefit of the doubt?

Giving someone the benefit of the doubt simply implies that even in tense situations, you are still willing to act favorably, put aside your negative opinions, and assume the best when you don't have all the information.

Love itself can be forgiving. It won't cause the mind to get saturated with unfavorable thoughts. Even after being proven wrong or experiencing disappointment, it will try to find a way around challenging circumstances.

Love "bears all things, believes all things, hopes all things, endures all things," as the Bible says. Love does not act foolishly; rather, it offers the benefit of the doubt. Love decides to find the best in others. This type of benefit is not something you just provide because you feel like it.

Most importantly, you choose to love your partner enough to give them the benefit of the doubt. This is a selfless deed. How then can you successfully extend the benefit of the doubt to your partner?

Love

The trick here is understanding how to love someone. Simply said, you cannot demand perfection from one person while also expecting them to accept you for who you are. This is not unconditional love. Selfishness, the foundation of conditional love, prevents you from giving someone the benefit of the doubt.

Patience

To find the truth and settle disputes, patience is required. Giving the benefit of the doubt does not include drawing hasty assumptions.

Understanding

It's crucial to try to imagine yourself in the other person's position. You never know; they can be hesitant to be themselves out of fear of being rejected, abandoned, or for any other reason. Before collaborating with your spouse on anything, just assume that they have made an effort to be sincere and grow with you.

Forgiveness

Learning to forgive and forget is the last thing you need, but it's certainly not the least. Never allow yourself to harbor resentment. Once you've managed to control your initial rage, keep it in the past and try not to let it interfere with your thoughts in the future.

CHAPTER 4

Modify Your "Blame Them" Attitude

Another major no-no in a relationship is placing the blame on the other person. It will never do you any good to let someone else take the responsibility for your mistakes. Discover how to alter this pessimistic outlook right now.

If you continually step over the other person's mistakes, your relationship won't be able to move forward.

Say it from the 'I' perspective rather than using blame-based rhetoric. Instead of saying, 'Well you're constantly leaving a mess in the house,' say, 'I feel that it makes me a bit angry when I see the mess in the house'.

Eliminate the Negative Blame in Your Relationship

When it comes to assigning blame in a relationship, it might be much simpler to recognize your partner's mistakes than your own.

Couples that accuse one another have one of the worst problems since, most of the time, both parties are incorrect. Every person has their shortcomings, and some of the ways they try to defend themselves result in their pushing other people away.

As you grow close to someone, your self-protective mechanisms become much more powerful since old emotions start to affect you in unexpected or even unconscious ways. Knowing and overcoming these defenses you have is crucial if you want to strengthen your relationship, make it thrive, and make it survive longer.

Why not consider your capabilities before adopting the blame-them mentality and preferring to concentrate on your partner's shortcomings?

Try not to make a case

When a disagreement begins, it is simple to add fuel to the fire by presenting many examples of your partner's weaknesses in character. One morning of accidentally overcooking the egg can already trigger a full-fledged argument that your partner should try to learn how to cook, in which you list every instance in which something similar has occurred.

One of the main problems in any partnership is case building. If you don't want your relationship to be always occupied with various situations, day in and day out, try to avoid doing this.

Consider leaving It

Who is really to blame won't be able to be determined once the blame has already started to shift and things have gotten out of hand. In reality, there is no winner in these disputes. The war is over even though the fight could have been won.

Just make an effort to remain focused on the essentials. It won't hurt to just let the past go, let your guard down, and be kind to one another if your goal is to get close once more.

The first step to restoring your relationship's loving and natural flow of emotions might be unilateral disarmament.

Be calm

Relationships can affect you in ways that you never anticipate. Things might trigger you easily, especially when your defenses are heightened. When you become provoked, attempt to concentrate and unwind before responding. Fighting with fire won't help you at all. Before approaching your partner, take some time to collect yourself. This will make managing their anger simpler.

Express Your Emotions

The time to communicate how you felt without feeling victimized or assigning blame is after you have calmed down and allowed your spouse to voice their perspective.

If you don't want things to get worse before they get better, refrain from making generalizations or speaking in a victimized manner. You give your relationship the best opportunity of continuing to be passionate, egalitarian, and rewarding once you shift your blame-them approach.

CHAPTER 5

Study Up On The Projecting Mindset

The projecting mindset is necessary even in partnerships. It is not sufficient to simply intend to take action. To assure the best for your relationship, you must remain steadfast and alter how you see the world. The following advice will help you adopt the proper perspective for your relationship.

Our perspective of what life is really about is significantly influenced by our thoughts and mindsets.

Your Relationship Will Make You Feel Right if You Have the Right Frame of Mind.

An inaccurately projected perspective can be harmful to both you and the relationship you are in. You will become a taker and a needy partner if you consistently believe that you have no cause to be loved by anyone and that others would leave you once they get to know you.

Before you realize it, your partner no longer wants to stand by your side, indicating that you are already correct. Naturally, you do not want this to happen, but if you keep depriving yourself of wonderful things, you will never be able to give or share since you will always feel empty within.

Good relationships are those that give and share, thus your relationship has no chance of being healthy if you continue to think negatively about it. Here are some suggestions to assist you in developing the proper projecting mindset that will improve your connection.

Never assume.

Expecting can lead you to unpleasant areas, which is regrettable. Assuming is detrimental and can be likened to a poison that can eat your thoughts. For instance, your previous relationship ended because your ex-partner had a habit of sending converse emails to others when you weren't looking. After that, you found another, and when you see your current partner checking email, you presume right away that they are the same as your former partner.

You jump in and make accusations when, in reality, the email is entirely business-related. It's crucial to remember that no two people are exactly alike, and your current relationship may not share the same faults as a former one.

Making snap judgments will cause your lover to leave you before you even realize it.

Live in the present moment.

It's not a good idea to try to live in the past or spend too much time thinking about the future. Some people became so mired in their history that it is practically necessary for them to still exist.

There are also others who have already planned out their entire life and live just for the future.

It's a wonderful idea to apply some significant lessons from your history to the present or to plan a trip you've been wanting to take for a while. Yet just as you shouldn't plan out every last aspect of the future, you should never allow the past to rule your present completely.

Making decisions based on the present rather than the past or what you hope to become in the future will allow things to fall into the appropriate places as they are designed.

Be Thankful

Being thankful for your life's blessings and your current situation is one of the keys to projecting the appropriate mindset. You may project more optimism into your life and prevent yourself from becoming overwhelmed by any challenges that may arise by giving thanks for the blessings that your partnership is currently experiencing.

As long as you and your spouse support one another in moving your relationship in the direction you want, projecting the appropriate mindset is simple.

CHAPTER 6

Increase Compassion

Being empathetic to one another is one of the essential elements of a good relationship. The best time for you to start learning how to reintroduce compassion into your relationship is when you feel like it is missing this one crucial component.

Relationships are about whether you see each other, not how you see each other.

A Relationship Characterized by Compassion Leads to Happiness

Compassionate individuals are happier individuals. Couples are more understanding and joyful in their relationships when they feel compassion for one another. Compassion is regarded as the cornerstone for people who desire to have a fulfilling love life. Compassion is the mixture of consideration, kindness, concern, and empathy.

The smallest act of compassion from your partner can already make a huge difference in how you feel when you're depressed and down. Any discomfort you might feel can already be eliminated by encouraging words and cuddly hugs. Any suffering, no matter what it may be about, may be readily alleviated by having someone to hold your hand and provide you with the emotional support you need by remaining by your side.

Partnerships without compassion are frequently abrasive. As a result, communication will become less compassionate, which can cause resentments to accumulate and make you feel as though you are the only one in the relationship.

Compassion development and expression can create a safe space for your love as well as other emotions and problems that may arise. Nothing can take the place of your partner's compassion or tenderness. The two of you can heal via this, and it will provide you the emotional comfort you never even realized you needed.

It is quite simple to develop compassion, and desire is the key component. Thus, it's crucial to first inquire about any wants your spouse may have before outlining your own. As a result of this debate, it will be simpler for you both to be compassionate toward one another because you both understand where your attention should be directed.

The second thing that could be a little difficult is committing to always maintain compassion in every conversation. A compassionate relationship is devoid of harshness, so when it does arise, the two of you need to immediately identify it and end it so that you may resume relating in a healthy way.

Looking into one other's eyes is a straightforward but powerful activity to increase compassion. Although this activity may have been overly glorified in movies, it rarely occurs in contemporary relationships. Instead of focusing intensely on the television, take a moment to slow down, look deeply into your partner's eyes, and feel the feelings that he or she is experiencing. This will help you to develop deeper empathy.

Being compassionate is preferable to just showing compassion. When your partner confides in you about an issue, and you express worry, you let them know that you will not only be there for them but that you also care about what they are going through. Your partner will experience it and will reciprocate your gesture in the same way that you did.

Make sure to develop and cultivate compassion as a vital component of your everyday love. Knowing that your lover loves you in the same manner you love them is one of the most tangible feelings in the world.

CHAPTER 7

Before You Talk, Adjust Your Mindset

Any relationship might suffer if the wrong words are said at the wrong moment. For the sake of not offending your spouse, it's best to consider things before you speak and blurt out what you're thinking. To adopt this mentality, there are some suggestions you can bear in mind.

Don't forget: Words have the power to break our hearts, not sticks and stones.

Choose Your Words Wisely and Carefully

Even the most basic words have the power to elicit loyalty, cheer up the soul, and transform lives. They have the power to revive the dead or mutilate hearts that were once whole.

Moreover, words have the power to destroy a character, alienate a soul, and display excessive generosity and brutality.

Thinking before you speak is essential in any relationship since words have amazing and occasionally destructive power.

Every relationship has its fair share of emotional sludge and unresolved problems, which can harm it. It is crucial to evaluate what you will say before you say it, as well as whether the words are coming from a loving and kind heart or a heart that flows with bitterness, hatred, anger, and other unproductive feelings. This will help ensure that your connection survives and thrives.

You can never take back words or phrases that have already left your mouth. There is no way to take back the words you said in the heat of an argument, no matter how hard you try to say something different or better or repair the harm caused by them. The harm has been done.

There is still hope, though, and it comes from thinking carefully before speaking.

One thing to keep in mind is to first think about the impact that your words might have on the other person. Will they feel horrible about it? Will it undermine their self-confidence? To prevent offending people's feelings, such considerations should be made.

Speaking requires timing, and you must always keep in mind that timing is everything. When you're stressed or feeling upset, refrain from speaking negatively. If you don't have enough time to talk things out, never start a conversation that is likely to be highly emotional.

Think about why you're speaking. Think twice before speaking if you only want to speak for the sake of speaking. Will the language be harsh? Should you just leave them unspoken and in their current state to prevent any awkward feelings? It's crucial to talk from genuine, honorable motivations.

Being thoughtful before you speak is essential in any relationship since you cannot take back what you have said. No matter how hard you try to mend a shattered heart, it will always remain broken.

CHAPTER 8

Keep Your Limits

Relationships, especially intimate ones, require boundaries. To keep healthy limits in the future and to have a successful relationship, learn how to set and uphold them for yourself.

We feel taken advantage of and abused when we don't establish limits and hold individuals responsible. Because of this, we occasionally criticize who they are, which is much more painful than addressing a behavior or a decision.

Setting Boundaries is Essential for Healthy Partnerships

Limits are a set of restrictions that reinforce your sense of independence and identity. These may be psychological, physiological, sexual, or spiritual. You decide whether to set them to defend yourself and demand respect. Boundaries can alter over time and differ from one relationship to the next.

Establish Your Limits

Take into account your likes and dislikes. Understand the behaviors, situations, and attitudes that make you uneasy. Knowing exactly what your limits are will help you establish them firmly and clearly and identify when they have already been crossed.

Be Clear About Your Limits in Communication

Set boundaries directly and understandably. You must identify the boundary concerns and acknowledge your sentiments with them by using "I" statements.

Develop a Reaction to Boundary Violations

Prepare a potential reply in case your boundaries are pushed. You might reaffirm your limitations and express regret for transgressing them.

Inform your partner of the repercussions of crossing your boundaries.

Set and Stick to Limits

Maintain your composure, adhere to your established boundaries, and enforce the intended consequences. Your partner will believe that it is acceptable for you if they break your limits again if you fail to enforce them.

Your wants, desires, and feelings will appear worthless, pointless, and insignificant if your partner disregards your limits or does not regard them seriously. To improve your relationship, talk to each other about your boundaries as this is unhealthy for any relationship.

CHAPTER 9

Affirmations might help you stay on track

Discover the various affirmations you may repeat to yourself each day to help you stay on track with your relationship resolution.

A properly positioned question mark can mean the difference between happiness and calamity when you're in love, while a properly placed period or ellipsis can stop all kinds of exclamations.

Affirmations for a Successful Relationship

The first and most important place to start when developing a good relationship is with you. This is fantastic because it means you have complete control over creating a loving and good atmosphere and doing your part to foster all the qualities that a healthy relationship needs to have.

Several affirmations can help you remain on track and maintain the level of health in your relationship that you desire.

- My partner and I are inseparable.
- I work hard to cultivate and nurture the love that my partner and I have for one another.
- My spouse and I are becoming more and more in love.
- I will do everything in my power to keep my relationship with my partner happy.
- I hold my partner in the highest regard.
- Anytime I'm with my lover, I can be wholly myself.
- I can express my demands and desires clearly.
- If necessary, I can set my boundaries.
- I always take my partner's viewpoint into account.

- I'll make an effort to build a solid bond with my companion.
- I'm going to make a great spouse someday.
- I'll treat my spouse with consideration and respect.
- With every day that goes by, my spouse and I become closer.
- I'm entitled to a fulfilling relationship.
- I believe it's crucial to pay attention to what my partner has to say.
- Honest communication is one of my skills. To me, any and every effort is worth it if it results in a happy and healthy relationship.

CHAPTER 10

Your Relationship Resolution's Advantages

Once you've arrived here, you've probably discovered just how much you can genuinely do to improve your relationship.

So what advantages may you anticipate from your relationship resolution?

The best approach to love someone, in my opinion, is to support them in being their best selves rather than trying to alter them.

When you make and keep your relationship resolution for the upcoming year and many years to come, there are many advantages that you will undoubtedly enjoy for the remainder of the year.

You're Sure to Have a Healthy Relationship

The path to preserving a healthy relationship is paved by relationship resolutions. When two people respect each other, stay true to who they are, and appreciate their spouse completely, that is when a good relationship is being built.

This will indeed involve respect, tolerance, and compromise, but it will still be worthwhile because everyone wants to connect on a deeper level with someone they love and feel secure in their most important relationships.

You can rebuild the connections and emotions that were severed along the way.

As the years go by and they appear to become too accustomed to being in each other's company, it is very normal for a long-term relationship to lose some sentiments and connections.

During a relationship resolution, you might have the ideal opportunity to find everything that has been lost and return it, or even better, take things a step further and transform your relationship from the inside out. It aids in reigniting the spark and reviving ancient fires that time seems to have doused without your knowledge.

You and Your Partner Both Develop as People. Your Benefit as Well as That of Your Relationship

The goal of relationship resolution is to enable the two parties to that relationship to discover their worth so they can become better for their partner and the others around them. This goal is more essential than simply saving the relationship itself.

This resolution can assist you in finding your path if you feel like you lost yourself during the relationship and help you recover, this time stronger than before.